From My Understanding

By: Reginald (Dunbar) Walton

From My Understanding

Reginald "Dunbar" Walton

From My Understanding

Poems by: Reginald "Dunbar" Walton

Front Cover Picture by: Reginald "Dunbar" Walton
Design by: Jazzy Kitty Publishing
Logo Designs by: Andre M. Saunders/Leroy Grayson
Editor: Anelda L. Attaway

© 2013 Reginald Walton
ISBN 978-0-9892656-3-8
Library of Congress Control Number: 2013945826

All rights reserved. This book is protected under the copyright laws of the United States of America. No part of this publication may be reproduced or transmitted in any format or by any means electronic, mechanical, or otherwise, including photocopying, recording or any other storage or retrieval system without written permission of the publisher, except in the case of brief quotations embodied in critical articles or reviews.

For Worldwide Distribution. Printed in the United States of America. Published by Jazzy Kitty Greetings Marketing & Publishing, LLC. Utilizing Microsoft and Adobe Publishing Software. Utilizing Adobe and Microsoft Publishing Software.

Other Books By Reginald Walton...

This Ain't A Joke

This Nigger Is Crazy

Coming Soon...

Hip Hop, Poetry & Spoken Word

Vibe

The Divine Book of Wisdom

Love is a Jewel

The Secret of the Wise

This Is Life

And More...

Dedications:

This book is dedicated to all those that came before me and to all that will come after me. Read the secrets I reveal to you and reach your own understanding.

Table of Contents:

Introduction	i
The Face in the Glass	01
Forever My Lady	03
Loving a Convict	05
Moving You	07
Beautiful	08
Rejoice!	09
The Greatest Gift God Could Send	10
"The Way"	12
What Did Yesterday Say?	13
"Boobaby"	14
In the Blink of an Eye	16
Slowly I'll	18
What Ever Happened?	19
Bettering Yourself	21
Resolution	23
Death	26
Stop Spreading Stress	28
To Be with You	29
Food for Thought	30
Praise & Worship	31

Table of Contents:

The Passion of the Christ	33
"Here We Go Again"	35
Love - A Funny Way of Showing Itself	37
One Face... Yours!	39
Love	40
Harsh Words	41
For Lost Souls	44
Making a Difference	47
Natures Course	48
Daddy's	50
Time is Precious	52
24-Hours a Day Friend	53
"Power to Grow"	54
Faith	55
When Evening Comes	56
A Brother's Love	57
A Brother's Love 2	58
It Cannot	59
"A Beautiful Thing"	60
To My Family and Friends	62
"Latoya"	64

Table of Contents:

"Poet's Cry" 65

"When a Man Loves a Woman" 66

Just for Today 67

Thank God 68

The Cure 69

United We Stand 71

For My Wife 72

Fallen Angel 73

Company You Keep 75

"Giddy" 78

"Bud" 78

"Momma" 81

Lovers 83

My Daughter 84

About the Author 85

Book Ordering Information 86

Introduction:

This book was solely inspired by a few inmates I was trapped in a concrete hell with back in 2003. Although all of these ideas originated from me, these inmates help me realize that I didn't have to take that path that I was headed on as my life's destination. They let me know that I had a world of talent in my hands and all I had to do was develop it; so I began to write and write and write. Every week I had something new on my plate. Blended perfectly with the sword of truth, and seasoned perfectly throughout the years: *This is* **FROM MY UNDERSTANDING!**

…Mr. Reginald "Dunbar" Walton.

THE FACE IN THE GLASS

When you get what you want
In your struggle for self
And the world makes you King for a day
Just go to a mirror and look at yourself
And see what **the face** has to say

For it isn't your father, mother, or spouse
Whose judgment upon you must pass
The person whose conduct counts
Most in your life is the one...
Staring back from **the glass**

Some people might think
You're a straight-shooting cum
And call you a wonderful guy or gal
But the **face in glass** says...
You're only a bum

If you can't look it straight in the eye
That's the one you must please
Never mind all the rest
For that's the one who's with you

Clear up to the end
You know you have passed
Your most dangerous test if
The face in the glass is your friend

You may fool the whole world down the pathway of life
And get pats on the back as you pass
But your final reward will be heartbreak and tears
If you're cheated **the face in the glass**

FOREVER MY LADY

My emotions get the best of me...
Whenever I see your beautiful face
I'm reminded of stolen moments
Hugs, kisses, and God's sweet grace

For some reason He sent you to me
Like a star shooting through the night
The billowing hair that flowed down your neck
Obviously, love at first sight

I imagine days of leaving my shop
To spend time enveloped in your embrace
Listening to the accounts of your day...
While kissing you upon your face

I imagine days of togetherness
From the beginning to the end of each day
I'd hate to see you have to leave
But I'd love to watch you walk away

You've been a friend to me throughout the years
And to you I owe my life
You were there when no one else cared
Thank God that you're my wife

O.K., you're not my wife yet
But I imagine that you are
But by giving me your hand in Holy Matrimony...
I'll be the happiest man from afar!

Make an honest man out of me
Let's go half on a life together
I'll scatter my dreams at your feet
To twinkle forever and ever

I will always love you…

LOVING A CONVICT

Loving a convict isn't as easy they say
Loving her is a high price to pay

It's loving without her to hold
It's keeping warm when feeling oh so cold

It's remembering the promises to wait
It's remembering the hopes you have made

It's knowing that she is far away
It's praying it won't be too long of a stay

Picturing walking the lonely yard
Picturing her always under a guard

Doing her best to fight off the clowns
Knowing she is able to hold her ground

Laying alone with all of your fears
Falling asleep with eyes full of tears

It's knowing more than anyone...
That life can be tough
For **loving a convict** is rough

But the woman I love is so true
Knowing if I wait, I will get what is due

It won't be forever that I'll have to wait
Soon enough she'll be coming thru the gate

Then **my convict** will be free
And a convict no more...
Is what she will be

MOVING YOU

Eight Birthday candles

Makes a very lonely light

But not as bright as your eyes tonight

Blow out the candles...

Make a wish come true

Forever I'll be wishing that I was there with you

You're only eight years old

But you're my little Queen

You're the prettiest little girl

My eyes have ever seen

Eight Birthday candles...

In my heart they will glow

Forever and ever more

For your uncle loves you so

I miss you...

BEAUTIFUL

You are more than just **beautiful**

You are my precious Queen

Compared to silver and gold...

You're my diamond ring

As the sun shines from over the mountain

It reflects your face up in the sky

If you ever take your love from me...

My soul will surely die

This is not a dream

Love is reality

Me minus you

I don't know where I'd be!

REJOICE!

When we celebrate this joyous season
Make sure it's for the right reason

Don't get caught up in the things of this day
We should praise Him...
The Truth, the Light, the Way

Celebrate the birth of His only Son
Through Him our lives with be won

We must **REJOICE**, no matter what
Whether we have, or whether we have not

Because on this day Our Savior was born
So glorify Him on Christmas morn

THE GREATEST GIFT GOD COULD SEND

In sin, we all seem to get lost

We want to have fun...

No matter the cost

We can try to go our own way

But it's with our life we will pay

We have to remember that the way to God

Is our path to find...

His love and direction will always be kind

What I want to seek is not mine

But His will

Through Him, I will have the greatest thrill

For Jesus, I will take a stand

I leave everything in His hands

Through His grace and mercy I will grow

This forever, will be all I...

Strive to know

Jesus will always be our Best Friend

To us He is...

THE GREATEST GIFT GOD COULD SEND

"THE WAY"

I feel so strong when You are near
With You by my side, I've nothing to fear

But I'd pray always that You
Remind me each day…
To always ask You to lead the way

Thank You Lord for blessing me so,
And bringing me safely through
Life's troubles and woes

For showing me the way home…To You of course

So please lead on my Lord…I humbly ask
Because with You I can face any task

Safe and sound in Your loving arms
Thank You Father for bringing me along
And keeping me safe from evil's harm

Thanks again for leading me today
And for always showing me the way

Amen

WHAT DID YESTERDAY SAY?

What did yesterday say?
It's hugs today and French kisses tomorrow
Could time be so smooth as to let me exist?
I'm seen as a weed, but I'm a yet bloomed garden

Yesterday said persevere...
Cause tomorrow's birth by today
Yesterday speaks to me through
Memorial passages

My passengers ride with me
Turn yesterday's volume up loud
Listen to its rhythm and heed

It's well pitched parable
Reverberated yesterdays
Embrace me in a melody
Of manifested touches intangible

As my tomorrow's become yesterdays
And my today's are sexed into yester morrows
I'm stagnated staring at life with eyes wide shut…

"BOOBABY"

Yesterday, just a mental photograph of yesterday

With all its edges folded like a fragile brown leaf

And yet, it's all I have of our past love

A postscript to its ending

Brighter days when every song we sang...

Is sung again

But this time with every intention of lasting forever

You've always been my **"Boobaby"**

You've always been near me...

Even from afar

I can remember our days,

When no one else mattered to me...But you

You were my Athena and I loved and adored you

The nights filled with joy was our Heaven

I pray that tomorrow brings you near me

I can recall my desire with every ounce of reverence

I had for you

Our love was a Spanish fiesta

To look in your eyes was my joy each day

The nights were the heart of yearning

The sound of our heartbeats together

Were like castanets,

And Eternally we'll know its true meaning

Still my sunshine,

"Bud"

IN THE BLINK OF AN EYE

In the blink of an eye,

She read its meaning

Analyzing Ebonics Scriptures

Her, what it be Baby

Could us be Baby?

Baby say just maybe

With every blink, she flipped a scroll

Losing control as she captured...It's subliminal

Intrigued by its criminal, it's lust she felt

As if, she was reciting a ghetto ritual

She convulsed of possibility

Could it be she's into thee?

Hmmmmm, maybe just uh,

Falling soul first into each

And every verse

She's on a midnight train
Destination I
I is what she imagines behind
Her open eyes

In an eye blink its meaning
Is what she read
It's subliminal is now what
Dances is her head

SLOWLY I'LL

Slowly creeping comes the habit
In Hell - yet still they grab it

Their hunger grows-
The only meal of the day
Slinging one - two - three
From down the way

Got a hold that's tight
Mind & body, too weak to fight
Every word nothing but lies
Their soul spits unheard cries

With all they have done
There is no love
The only place to find it...
Is up above

Don't end up broken filled with hate
Jailhouse Junkie, get your life straight
You too can rise...Above all
Everyone is not meant to fall

WHAT EVER HAPPENED?

What Ever Happened...
To the love that we once shared?

What Ever Happened...
To all the things that you'd do
Just to show me that you cared?

What Ever Happened...
To that smile that used to shine so bright?

And **What Ever Happened...**
To the kiss that we would share
Before saying goodnight?

These are just some of the things
Between us that I really miss
And if I was to wake up holding you in my arms
I know my heart would be filled with bliss

I pray that things could be different
Because without you...I feel all alone inside
I tend to wrap myself in my loneliness
Because that's the only...Place I know to hide

Now with all this being said

I guess I'll bring this message to an end

But until all my questions are answered

I'll continue to ask myself…

"What Ever Happened?"

BETTERING YOURSELF

I sit and wonder why I couldn't
Have done things **better**,
But truly I have no one to blame
For why I've **not done better…**

All the pain and frustration
I've pushed out in my life
I can never stand
For I should keep my head up
To make that change…

I take one day at a time from here
On out and should never doubt myself
From this point on…

So long as I keep my head up and
Strive to stay strong and keep
It all together, **I will do better…**

Maintaining a life of good and not evil
Will make you feel much better…

(Proverbs 19:20)
Listen to advice and accept instruction,
and in the end you will be wise…

On top of it all though,
Remember that life is what you make it…

God Bless All

RESOLUTION

Just for today,

I will live through this day only

I will not broad about tomorrow

I will not set far-reaching goals

Or try to overcome all my problems at once

I know I can do something for 24 hours...

That would overwhelm me...

If I had to keep it up for a lifetime

Just for today,

I will be happy

I will not dwell on thoughts...

That will depress me

If my mind fills with clouds

I will chase them away and fill it with sunshine

Just for today,

I will accept what is

I will correct those things I can correct

And accept those I cannot

Just for today,

I will improve my mind

I will read something that

Requires effort and concentration

I will not be a mental loafer

Just for today,

I will make a conscious

Effort to be more agreeable

I will be more open minded

I will be kind and courteous

To those who cross my path

And I will not speak ill of others

I will not look down on those

Who are less fortunate

I will speak softly...

And not interpret others

I will refrain from improving anybody...

But myself

Just for today,
I will do something
Positive to improve my health
If I'm not satisfied weight
I'll eat healthy and exercise

Just for today,
I will mend with
Those I've wronged

Just for today,
I will do what's right
And take responsibility for my own actions

Just for today,
I will seek **"God"**
With an open mind and heart
And let Him guide me through...
The Year!

DEATH

Death awaits you from a place

Unseen, and beckoning

He waits patiently...time is on his side

Each day that passes...

He creeps closer and closer,

Each breath brings him nearer

His approach, approach through well known

To all, is despised and unwelcome

By most, except souls who have prepared for his arrival

Their souls have been washed...

By their tears, standing & kneeling at night,

Crying out and begging for redemption

In the deepest, darkest part of the night

They ponder upon their deeds,

Beating on their chests about the good deeds that escaped

Then that day, crying about their faults

While others cling to the warm comforts of their beds

Yes, **death** awaits you;
He will not warn you
And seize you by your forelock;
Lying, sinful forelock

At a time when you are ready
But this will not matter
For your appointed time with him
Cannot be pushed back
Nor can it be propelled forward

Even if it was your ardent desire
Laying in the clutches of **death**
The pure soul yields itself up...
Freely, effortlessly

Happy to meet his Creator and
His Creator happy to meet him
However, the unwilling soul resists,
Struggles, panic-stricken,
It claws and clutches, not yet ready
Unhappy to meet its Creator and
Its Creator unhappy to meet it

STOP SPREADING STRESS

Why can't we all be happy?
And not cause others **stress**
We need to count each day alive
And realize we are blessed!

If something bad happened for you
Don't make others pay
What does it take to give a smile
And pleasant things to say?

Life certainly has ups and downs
That we all must go through
But the day would certainly go better
With a kind of bitterness from you

TO BE WITH YOU

I once had a heart and it was true
Through now, I have none...And you have 2

I ask you to forgive me
For the things that I have done
Girl, I was young minded...It was all in fun

Now if I die before you get there
I'll carve your name in a golden stair
So that my heart can be free from despair

If I cannot hear you sing
I'll give the angels back their wings
Their golden hair and all those things

So if you are not there on Judgment Day
I'll know you went the other way
So I'll tear down the Gates of Heaven that day

When the chance comes and I am through
Just know that I would go through
The depths of Hell...**Just to be with you**

FOOD FOR THOUGHT

You would be amazed
At how much thinking
On top of thinking
And rethinking of thought…

One can do, when one has
Nothing but "TIME" to do just that
So, before you get up and go…

Try to take a moment to
"STOP AND THINK" about where:
At, in, or to what place
Situation, position, direction,
Circumstances, or respect…
You are going…

(Food for thought)

PRAISE & WORSHIP

The Word of God says;

Make a joyful noise unto the Lord

And one can't do this

If that one is always feeling bored

Even if we had a thousand tongues

We could never thank God enough

So why not **praise** Him today

Because of His grace - life is not rough

I **praise** Him because I'm happy

And I **worship** Him because I'm glad

He saved me from the Devil's grip

And never again will I be sad

I give all glory to the Lord my God

An audience of One

His name is JESUS CHRIST

And oh yeah, He's God's Son!

I sing for Him

My wife Angela dances for Him

And our baby-girl Amira smiles for Him

And the three of us together

Take the Gospel above the rim

Hallelujah is the highest praise

To Him all Honor is due

I'm gonna **praise** Him until I die

Which is why **worship** is true

THE PASSION OF THE CHRIST

The Passion of the Christ is the movie
That everyone needs to see
It's a movie about the last 12 hours
Of a Man, who died for the sins of you & me

The Passion of the Christ
Is what the critics were all talking about
Just when you thought everyone in Hollywood was stupid
They knew enough not to stop this movie...
From coming out!

While filming the crucifixion scene
The actor playing Jesus got quite a shock
Oh yeah, he got struck by lightning
Showing him that God is watching...
From up top

So if you haven't got a ticket to see it
Go out and get one now
If you hurry,
You can catch the anointing from on high...
That's coming down

The Passion of the Christ is the story
Of a wonderful and special Man
Who loved mankind so much that
He decided to die for him & take a stand

He took a stand against Satan
And the many wages of sin
So that in the end we could have "VICTORY"
And know that God will always win

The Passion of the Christ
Made $26 Million in its first day
Made the Devil & his demons are real mad
Proving that true deliverance
Is here to stay!!!

"HERE WE GO AGAIN"

Extended Visiting time is here again

And I can't wait to see you

I had such a nice time last October

That the memory of it has reminded true

You were looking extremely wonderful

In the outfit, you had chosen to wear

Straight off the cover of Ebony magazine

I couldn't help but to look and stare

We talked a lot about the anointing

The Lord has placed over our marriage

It reminds me of us riding thru the park

Is a horse-driven rose pedaled carriage

The Lord has indeed blessed us Angela

From our head to the soles of our feet

I am forever thankful for that special day

He allowed us to come together & meet

Here we go again, yet one more time
Desiring to be in each other's company
We always make the best of each moment
Because we're both vessels in God's family

Love Always

LOVE - A FUNNY WAY OF SHOWING ITSELF

Why does love have a funny way of showing itself?
I wonder does love have wealth?

"Yes" it does - the ability to love!
Love…Such a strong word to use -
Also a powerful word to abuse

When a loved one is down
Why does the other take advantage?
Was love ever grounded
"Or" just taken for granted?

Do we love?
Or, maybe it is
Desires deep down inside
Maybe it's a word to say you're
In for the long ride

Can love get so deep
You can put it in words
Yet you shed tears when it's heard
Can love get so strong

It blinds us from reality, some
It messes up their mentality

Some get physically beaten
Stripped of their dignity - mentally
Spiritually weakened, all because
Of this love worked we're speaking

Without love
We wouldn't understand hate
Love, sometimes it gives
Sometimes it takes
But when we love, do we appreciate?

Why when we love
Do we creep to someone else?
Cause love has...
A funny way of showing itself!

ONE FACE...YOURS!

If there's **One Face** I want to see

Each day my whole life through

One Smile that makes a difference

In everything I do

If there's **One Touch** I long to feel

One Voice I long to hear

Whenever I am happy or just

Needing someone near…

If there's **One Joy**

One Love from which

I never want to part…

It's YOU -

That someone special

In my world, my life, my heart

LOVE

Love has many powers:
It can bring you to your knees
Love can rip your heart like paper;
Then mend it back with ease

Love can bring out tears of sadness
And also tears of joy
Love can make us smile at someone
Who's trying to annoy
Love is all around us

No matter where we turn
Love can be so simple;
Yet heard for us to learn

Love has many powers:
As I have said above
But the most important thing of all is,
"You are my only Love."

HARSH WORDS

I ran into a stranger as he passed by
"Oh excuse me please," was my reply
He said, "Please excuse me too, I wasn't watching for you."

We were very polite, this stranger & I
We went on our way saying good-bye

But at home a difference is told
How we treat our loved ones
Young and old

Later that day, cooking the evening meal
My son stood beside me very still

As I turned, I nearly knocked him down
"Move out of the way!"
I said with a frown

He walked away...His little heart broken
I didn't realize how **harshly** I'd spoken

While I lie awake in bed

God's still small voice came to me and said,

"While dealing with a stranger common courtesy you use.

But the children you love, you seem to abuse.

Go and look on the kitchen floor,

You'll find some flowers by the door

Those are the flowers, he brought for you.

He picked them himself: Pink, yellow and blue.

He stood very quietly not to spoil the surprise

And you never saw the tears that filled his little eyes."

By this time, I felt very small

And now my tears began to fall

I quietly went and knelt by his bed;

"Wake up, little one, wake up," I said.

"Are these the flowers you picked for me?"

He smiled, "I found 'em out by the tree.

I picked 'em because they're pretty like you

I knew you'd like 'em...Especially in blue."

I said, "Son, I'm very sorry for the way I acted today;

I shouldn't have yelled at you that way."

He said, "Oh, Dad, that's okay. I love you anyway."

I said, "Son, I love you too. And I do like the flowers...
Especially the blue."

FOR LOST SOULS

How many people even dream of God?

What would it be to walk by His side!

A way to please Him

And love Him so much

A personal relationship to stay in touch

The world has lied

And looked for a fix

But the real truth of the author

Is in John 14:6

People wanna believe in God,

The way they are fit

Looking in the natural

To see what they could get

God is love and has One Spirit

You need Thee Lord JESUS

To be able to bear it

If you get saved
And seek God with a pure heart
Your eyes will be opened
And sin will begin to depart

The truth does hurt
And it will set you free
It will be revealed
If you really seek Thee

So ask yourself, "Do I wanna serve God
Or serve my own mind?"
People wake up!!!!!!
Satan has you blind

Lucifer pimps you
And you don't even know
But if you got the Holy Ghost
It will really show

I tell you the truth
Out of a heart of love, men
I would like to see you all
In Heaven above

Life is short and

You are only a breath

Do you have assurance...

Where you will go beyond death?

No Jesus, No Peace.

Know Jesus, Know Peace

MAKING A DIFFERENCE

What I want most in life
Is to fulfill a special need…
To **make a lasting difference**
Without arrogance or greed

To reach out to another
And touch a heart in pain…
To help them find their way
And see them smile again

It's God who does the healing
Not our own abilities…
He uses us as vessels to bring others to their knees

Without His strength and power
Our deeds are all in vain…
But God is all sufficient
And His love heals all the pain

Each life we touch is precious
Because God's hand is on us too…
As we reach out to another
It's God, not me or you

NATURES COURSE

Stars shine bright on a clean dark night
While lying in my bed my mind takes plight

I journey to a place in the distant far away
And dream of you from the place where I lay

I see a woman, so sleek and agile
I stop in my tracks to stare for a while
And contemplate…

I proceed on farther to the task at hand
I must reach you, it is my demand

The road is straight and narrow
No curves or bend
I finally reach you my Queen
With hair blowing in the wind

You stare at me
As if you already know;
I stare back at you
And say, "Here we Go."

We fall down gently
On the lush, green grass
My hand travels south
And starts rubbing your ass

I start to undress you
With my gentle touch
Your smiling at me;
You like it so much

I caress your whole being
Then we start to kiss
You say not a word
But start grinding your hips

In turn, we switch places
Now it's your game
I cannot tell a lie,
I like it the same

We tear into each other with no remorse
And with that we let
Nature Take Its Course

DADDY'S

Daddy decided to write this poem
With a warm heart and open arms
I love you more than words can say
I can't wait to come home

So we can have fun and play
Learning about each other
Is gonna make my day
And I'll be smiling all the way

Daddy's got your picture on his wall
And to me - you are the "best"
Kids of them all!

Kissing your picture helps me
Deal with my situation
If I could, I'd be there with no hesitation

Daddy's not perfect
And he wants you to see
Traveling down this path
Ain't no place to be

I love and miss you so much
No matter where I'm subject to be
You will always be
The best part of me!

TIME IS PRECIOUS

If there's a deed you left undone

Before the setting of the sun

Do it now!

If there's words you didn't speak

To soothe the hurt or boost the weak

Do it now!

If you can make a sick friend well

Or just a happy story to tell

Do it now!

Time is precious every day

Make it count in an unselfish way

24-HOURS A DAY FRIEND

Isn't it wonderful to have

A **24-hours a day friend**

That is there with you from beginning to end

Always an open ear to hear your prayer

He walks beside you everywhere

When you're burdened down and out

He will comfort you without a doubt

Keeping you in perfect peace

With such a joy...

So life struggles you can defeat

He loves you...Cares for you

Protects you unconditionally!

This is why I feel so happy; so free!

Jesus, I love You

You're so good to me

Forever I'll walk with You into Eternity

"POWER TO GROW"

At this moment I do not know
Just how this trial will make me grow

I searched Your Word and seek Your Voice
For from You alone...
True wisdom will come forth

So as I pass through this trial in life
Strengthen me Lord to carry on
Knowing that You know what's best
Helping me to remember that
My joy is found in Your eternal rest

Though I may not see right now
Please O Lord, show me how

That I may grow through these hours
And let it be to Your glory that I sing
For You have shown me through Your mercy and grace
When God is the Gardener...**I can grow any place**

FAITH

Faith is believing in the unbelievable
Faith is believing in what you can't see
Faith is believing that anything is possible
For **faith** let the Lord walk upon the sea

Ask the Father in the name of the Lord
And you will be granted all your needs
Show the world your **faith** in the Word
And the Lord will help you plant a good seed

Worry and doubt are the seeds of evil
Growing weeds in the heart of faithless minds
So practice your **faith** & strengthen your will
Leaving all your worries & doubts behind

WHEN EVENING COMES

Evening is a time to think
Your own thoughts clearly through
A time to cuddle little ones
And for them to cuddle you

Evening is a time to sit
Write a letter to a friend
A time to be for family
To visit, sew or mend

Evening is a time to sleep
And do so without any fear
For knowing God's working day & night
To answer to every prayer

A BROTHER'S LOVE

Today is a day especially for you
To show you how much you are
Appreciated & mean so much to me

I say Happy Birthday
From the heart
But to let you know also -
That you're my heart

There are so many things
We've done together
But what God has given us
Will last a lifetime and that is love

So always know that you
Are special in every way
And just to see you smile
Makes my day!

A BROTHER'S LOVE 2

Today is a special day for you
And I want you to know
How much you mean to me

Remember things we did
Growing up together
Time has surely flown by

I used to look up to you
Now I'm taller than you
But most of all
I thank God for you

So I wish you a Happy Birthday
Full of joy ever after
So always know that
You are "SPECIAL" in every way
And like I said earlier…
Just to see you smile makes my day!

Wishing you a HAPPY BIRTHDAY!

IT CANNOT

Cancer is so limited…

It cannot cripple God's Love,

It cannot shatter Hope,

It cannot corrode Faith,

It cannot eat away Confidence,

It cannot destroy God's Peace,

It cannot kill Friendship,

It cannot suppress Memories,

It cannot silence Courage,

It cannot invade the Soul,

It conquer the Spirit,

It cannot lesson the power of the Resolution,

And it cannot steal God's gift of Eternal Life!

"A BEAUTIFUL THING"

Whenever I find myself thinking about you

A smile always comes across my face

And I thank [God] for allowing me to be able to...

Display some "JOY" in this place

Angela, nothing makes me more happier

Than to sit and reminisce about you

I also would like to thank the Lord for you

For all the wonderful things that you do

For example, you're always

Encouraging me to stay strong

And you constantly remind me to pray

And even though I'm away right now

I thank [God] for giving you the strength to stay

Angela, a heart like yours belongs in a museum...

For the whole wide world to see

I know it is nothing special I have done

That empowers you to continue to be with me

So no matter what the future may hold

With [Jesus] inside of me - I'll be there

But if for some reason I'm not home -

Before our Savior's return

Thanks for showing me a love

That's most definitely beyond compare

TO MY FAMILY AND FRIENDS

There are times in our lives and I've seen quite a few
When the road up ahead seems too hard to get through

But when you've got **friends** beside you,
Though the Lord seems far away
He is there within their lives for you
And that's why I have to say

Your prayers have made a difference in my life;
They've given me a peace in the darkest of nights

When it seemed I'd needed a miracle to relieve my heavy load
I felt my burdens lift gently raised by the hand of God

Your love has made a difference in my heart;
It's like a healing balm poured an each broken part

Now forgiven and forgiving, free from all that had me bound
No root of bitterness can spring up to despoil God's ground

Your witness has made a difference in my walk
Filled with sincerity...Not just vain or empty talk

And my brothers and sisters in the Lord
You are all my **friends**
God's special gift to me
Keeping me faithful to the end

Sometimes when God seems so distant
The world much too cruel to bear
I look for **friends**; I can turn to you because you are there!

And my fears, my doubts,
My sorrows disappear as the morning dew
For your prayers, your love, your witness,
Are gifts from the Lord, through you

I thank God for you!

"LATOYA"

You R the omega of my heart
The foundation 4 my conception of love
When I think of what a Black Woman should be
It's U that I think of

U will never fully understand
How deeply my heart feels 4 U
I always worried that we'd grow apart
And I'd end up losing U

Toy, U bring me 2 climax without sex
And you do it all with regal grace
Latoya R. Perkins, U R my heart
In human form...A Friend I could never replace
And I won't...I promise

"POET'S CRY"

It has always been easy to get to my heart
There is no other way of stating it the best poet's are lovers
And are receptacles for pain, joy, and injustice
And the innocent smiles of children we trust

Too early and easily we read potential in
The countless faces of evil
And we carry many, many wounds
We are often crippled yet, some heal quickly

Only to open their hearts to stories our children
Can see through the right words can send us on
Unlimited journeys the hurt in children's eyes
Releases fury in our souls & fists
Black girls mistreated and life brings tears

I do not wish it to always be this way
To care too much can damage
One's spirit, yet, the secret to the longevity
Of significant poets is:
We never give up on love, poetry, and the smiles...
Of the young

"WHEN A MAN LOVES A WOMAN"

On this day,

When our magnificence

Is immeasurable we are,

Beloved, simply this:

Two souls laid bare before ourselves

Before each other…

Before God,

And this is what defines

Us as beautiful...

Forever

JUST FOR TODAY

Just for today, my thoughts will be on Jesus
Living and enjoying life without the bondages of sin

Just for today, I will have faith in JESUS
Who loves me and enables me to walk in the Spirit

Just for today, I have the Word of God
I will try to obey it to the best of my ability

Just for today, through the Bible I will try
To get a better perspective of who I am in Christ Jesus

Just for today, I will be unafraid
My thoughts will be on family, the Body of Christ
People who have been redeemed
By the precious Blood of the Lamb
And have received Eternal Life

So life as I follow Jesus Christ
I have nothing to lose

THANK GOD

I sit here and think and I must say
I have to **thank God** for yet another day
Although normally my situation may seem kind of bleak
A new way of living is what this "God's Man" seeks

I've put the fast living and the thug life behind
Now a new way of life is what I will find

It may seem boring, this new life I've claimed
But I'm living a beautiful life
And I'm not feeling any shame

Things could be worst
I could be dead, buried 6 feet in the ground
But God in all His goodness...
Saw fit to turn my life around

People who love me
The ones I've hurt in the past
They all told me that life I was living...
Wouldn't last

THE CURE

It was cool out this morning

The ground was covered with dew

A wet misty fog,

Blocked most of the view

This place has a certain beauty..

At this hour of the day

But when the sun rises, the beauty all goes away

This place that I speak of is prison

And it's not a pretty place

Over two thousand different people

And not a smile on any face

I know I don't belong here or how long I must stay

I've asked the Lord to help me...

I'm sure He knows the way

Is it that I'm a bad person or is it that they just don't care?

God give me the answer...

At this point I'm unaware

A sudden warmth then lifted my body
The Lord's presence I'm sure
Like disease my sins were lifted
The Lord Jesus was my **cure**

So now I understand fully
And I see exactly what they meant
The sinful evil person I use to be
In Jesus name' I totally resent

I thank God everyday now
For keeping His hold on me
Because the love of His Son
Is finally, what truly set me free

UNITED WE STAND

My Sweet, you are the sun that warms my night
The glow that chases away the blues...
And makes my woes all right

So what, you're miles away...
Unable to feel my touch
But this doesn't affect the love that we share so much

For absence makes the heart grow fonder
Beyond any stretch of thought
I don't have to be the King of the world
I'm pleased with being the King of your heart

My Queen, we have begun a legacy that no force can hinder
The hideaways that we shared each day
Are perfect thoughts to remember

To say that I love you can go without saying
For love embodies my heart for you
So that you'll always be **united with me**
For what God has given me, I give to you
Please be my wife, for the rest of our lives

FOR MY WIFE

After all my years of living you
I still don't have a way to
Tell you how much happiness
You give me everyday -
After all my years of loving you
I don't know what I'd do

If I were feeling down sometimes
And could not turn to you -
After all my years of loving you

You are like a part of me
And I know that for a lifetime
I'll be wanting us to be sharing
With each other...Doing everything together -
After all these years I know that
I'll be loving you forever

I love you!

FALLEN ANGEL

There isn't one moment that passes
In which I don't think of you
Everywhere I look, there's your face
That beautiful smile follows me
All over the place

I have a photographic picture of you
Stored in my memory bank
The way you walk...You're my top model
My Mrs. America, my everything
Is this a dream or reality?

Please don't wake me
Because all my love is for you
You're the only one I want in my life
My beautiful Queen

If loving you is wrong
I'm guilty of committing a crime
And I sentence my to Love for an Eternity
How could I not love you
When you're more sweeter than Honey to a bee

We may not be perfect & that's a fact
But through trial and tribulation
I still got your back

When you become angry over things that take place
Still I recognize sweetness on your lovely face

Baby, cross your legs, and sit down in your chair
So I can relax you by playing in your hair

I know what you like,
And I'm here to please every little aspect
Of your desire and needs

Scientist studies the natural...
Phenomenon of the sun, moon, and stars
What Scientist has not yet recognized is that...
"HEAVEN" is missing **an angel** because...
You're here with me

COMPANY YOU KEEP

It is better to be alone, **than in the wrong company**
Tell me who your best friends are,
And I will tell you who you are

If you run with wolves, you will learn how to howl
But, if you associate with eagles,
You will learn how to soar to new heights

"A mirror reflects a man's face, but what he is really like
is shown by the kinds of friends he chooses."

The simple but true fact of life is that you become like
Those with whom you closely associate -
For the good and the bad

The less you associate with some people,
The more your life will improve
Anytime you tolerate mediocrity in others,
It increases your mediocrity

An important attribute in successful people is their impatience
With negative thinking and negative Acting people

As you grow, your associates will change
Some of your friends will not want you to go on
They will want you to stay where they are
Friends that don't help you, will want you to crawl

Your friends will stretch your vision or choke your dream
Those that don't increase you will eventually decrease you

Consider this:

- Never receive counsel from unproductive people.
- Never discuss your problems with someone incapable of contributing to the solution, because those who never succeed themselves are always first to tell you how. Not everyone has a right to speak into your life. You are certain to get the worst of the bargain when you exchange ideas with the wrong person.
- Don't follow anyone who's not going anywhere. With some people you spend an evening; with others, you invest it.
- Be careful where you stop to inquire for directions along the road of life.
- Wise is the person who fortifies his life with the right friendships.

Happy moments? **PRAISE GOD!**

Difficult moments? **SEEK GOD!**

Quiet moments? **WORSHIP GOD!**

Painful moments? **TRUST GOD!**

Every moment? **THANK GOD!**

If you see people without a (smile) today…
Give them one of yours

PEACE!

"GIDDY"

You are the glue that bonded my fragmented heart
The elation to which there is no end
The clearest string on a cherubim's harp
The shot of Sprite in Seagram's Gin

A mountain in Tanzania with a snow capped peak
My "Corazon Saint Maria" with chubby size 9 ticklish feet

That "Body by Jake" that we annihilated
Was our virtual "Rolls Royce" in love with you I participated

Because of who you are, I had no choice
Because you delighted every part of me
From my Duke curled hair to my country toes;
You touched the very heart of me

Just the thought of you brings sweet response…
Forcing my mind to forget you
Means denying the love
I've felt for you…Through the years

"BUD"

Because you're my best friend,

And the love we share is so very special;

I think it's only fair that I tell you how I feel

And what Happens when I…Think of you

I remember times of holding you close

Sharing a love that's far too advanced for most

I remember the feel of your hands as they caressed my face

And the way you hold me in a soul searching embrace…

When I look at you...

I see my world opening up right before my eyes

The magic I see in yours, is what holds me captivated…

I'm facing a loving man, wise far beyond his years

And I witness all of this through the happiness of my tears…

When I touch you...

I get a tingling sensation that rushes through me

I feel the loving arms, that keeps and holds me safe,

Constantly…

My hands go weak, and I get all giddy inside
It's that being-in-love-with-you-feeling
That keeps me on a high…

When I'm near you…
All the world I've known before, silently fades away
I'm holding on tight to you Jonathan, my Love,
So you won't stray

Our entire world of love seems a fantasy…
Even a dream

I've fallen very much in love with you, to a point…
I can't deny that when I look, touch & think of you,
Your nearness sends me on a cloud way past nine…

Written by: Shannon T.

"MOMMA"

You are the root of my true happiness
Without you, I would not exist

Momma, you are the backbone of the universe
Just like the sun is placed in the center of the solar system
And the moon & stars are placed around the sun

Momma, you symbolize earth, the vehicle of life,
And everything exists because of you
Just like the earth produces beautiful flowers
That blossom into something special

When the seed was planted into the fertile womb,
You gave birth to something special
And I am an extension of you and he
I still remember when I was a child
And before going to bed at night
You would thank God for your blessing
And end it with a prayer...
Always content with what little was there

Although **Mother's Day**
Comes only once a year
I love you all year round
To me every day is **"Mother's Day"**

To end my message with one last thought
Momma, you are the foundation of life
And the true meaning of love and happiness

Enjoy your day!!!

LOVERS

I always smell like sawdust

Hair curlin around my cap

Sun-squinted eyes, laughin' warm,

Left arm huggin' the ol' black dinner bucket

With the missin' handle

I stand wide-legged quiet

In her 5 o'clock kitchen

Close breathin' the back of her neck

Holdin' her hard, rubbin' her in ways

And places only a husband should

She leans back unable to breathe

Wanting to unzip my stretched

Cotton 501's, she in a housewife dress

Slidin' her brown leg 'tween

My jeaned thigh and unbutton

My 5 buttons, she sighs,

Whispers with a quick kiss, stop; behave

Suppers almost done

With a slow step back

I smile turn off the stove

'cause suppa can wait…

MY DAUGHTER

Amira, there are so many things a man may wish to be

& many things he would like to have

But only a few are as lucky as me

To have a wonderful **daughter** who is as special as you

You are **my daughter** Amira

And **my daughter** you will always be

No matter where I am or what I do

You can be sure I'm thinking of you

You bring my life joy and you are my greatest hope

In you, I see the brightest future and I know what you can do

So be strong for me Amira

And don't let this life bring you down

And remember your father

And always remember what I said

Now **my daughter,**

There's just one more thing I need to say

I love you so much in every possible way

Love Always Daddy!

About the Author...

Reginald Walton was born in Portsmouth, Virginia, and immediately moved to Baltimore where he grew up. He spent his childhood traveling up and down the East Coast and never stayed in one neighborhood for more than 1 year at a time. By the age of 9, he gravitated toward a life of crime. At the age of 15, he was charged as an adult for an attempt to murder. There he was - a child incarcerated with a bunch of grow men that society considered the worst of the worst, but they saw the potential in him and began to teach him. He would listen attentively and decided to make a change. The rest is in his writings. I hope you enjoy.

To Order Books From...

Jazzy Kitty Publishing Inc.

Call 877-782-5550

Or Email a request to anelda@jazzykitty.net

DESCRIPTION	UNIT PRICE
From My Understanding by Reginald Walton	$12.99
This Ain't A Joke by Reginald Walton	$12.99
This Nigger is Crazy by Reginald Walton	$12.99
The Psalms of Joseph Ashe Vol. 1 by Joseph Ashe Sr	$13.99
My Mind On Jesus: Incarcerated But I am Free by Joseph Ashe Sr.	$13.99

Shipping & Handling is not included:
Cost is based on the shipping address.

Please allow 21 days for personal checks to clear before receiving your order. Thank you!

www.ingramcontent.com/pod-product-compliance
Lightning Source LLC
Chambersburg PA
CBHW071833290426
44109CB00017B/1812